Here
or
Nowhere

Renée Hermanson

The Upper Room
Nashville, Tennessee

Here or Nowhere

Scripture quotations not otherwise identified are from *The New English Bible*, © The Delegates of the Oxford University Press and the Syndics of the Cambridge University Press 1961 and 1970, and are reprinted by permission.

Scripture quotations designated RSV are from the Revised Standard Version of the Bible, copyrighted 1946, 1952, and © 1971 by the Division of Christian Education, National Council of the Churches of Christ in the United States of America, and are used by permission.

Scripture quotations designated AP are the author's paraphrase.

Acknowledgment of other material quoted in this book can be found on pages 126-127.

Book Design: Harriette Bateman
Cover Design: Pat Van Atta
Cover Photograph: Bill Ross/West Light
First Printing: May, 1984 (7)
Library of Congress Catalog Card Number: 83-51401
ISBN 0-8358-0478-X

Printed in the United States of America

To Sheldon
Partner in all my Presents

Contents

Preface

Writing a second book is like having a second child. I know how long gestation takes and how hard it is to wait for new life to grow. I know, too, the pain and strain involved in delivering that new life into the world. There are both joy and anxiety in the anticipation.

This "pregnancy" was, like the times I waited for my babies to be born, a time that belonged mostly to me. Husband, relatives, and friends share in the expectation of a birth, just as my family and friends now wait to see "what she wrote this time." But all the happening has happened inside me. (I have a quasi-superstition that if I talk about it, I might not write it.)

When I was carrying our sons, I was constantly aware of the miracle growing within me. I was *responsible* for that life, but I was not forming or developing it. I could aid that growth by feeding my own body and giving it proper rest and exercise, but I could not decide the baby's sex, size, or personality or what impact that child would have on its world.

This book has been growing in me for several years.

The labor was mercifully short—I had a deadline—but there were anxious moments when I feared things were being forced to move too quickly. Through it all, I looked to the One in whom my life is grounded, realizing that while I was *responsible* for the work, I was as dependent on that Author for its growth and completion as I was for bringing my babies to term.

I have been, even aside from biological and literary pregnancies, a constant caller at the gate of grace. So much so, in fact, that sometimes I feared I was using up my portion, that someday the Keeper of the gate would say, "No more." Instead, I always found the gate open wide, ready to restore my wavering confidence and to supply my deepest needs. For this labor, I was given time away from regular employment and an environment in which to work that was at the same time stimulating and tranquil. My cup overflowed.

Now that this child of my reflection has been delivered, it is ready to be shared. I pray it will be to its readers what a child can sometimes be to an adult—an agent of revelation and newness. Children do not pretend to be profound or deep, but in their simplicity often rests a wisdom and a knowing that can unlock the secret places of our hearts. It is the Advocate, the Spirit of truth, who teaches everything, but sometimes a little child may lead us.

This book was written, then, that all "may hold the faith that Jesus is the Christ, . . . and that through this faith you may possess eternal life by his name" (John 20:31)—here and now.

John Netherton

Here and now I will do a new thing;
   this moment it will break from the bud.

—Isaiah 43:19

Here Is Newness

Pablo Picasso once commented that it takes a very long time to become young. I think I understand what he meant because it has taken me a very long time to become new.

I spent years doing it backward. As a child, I waited impatiently to be grown up. As an adolescent, I couldn't wait for the newness of womanhood to wear off so I could look sophisticated and older. I never did manage to look sophisticated, but I did get older. And still that elusive sense of having arrived escaped me. When I was in my twenties, I thought it might happen when I was thirty. Then I waited for the magic moment of life's beginning at forty. Whatever it was I was searching for—to know with solid certainty who I was and why I was and what my life was all about—remained just out of reach. It was never far away, never an impossible dream. It was always just over the next ridge, just beyond the misty veil, just past my reaching fingertips.

I had not, you understand, been spending all of my time during those years searching for myself. That quest was wedged between learning to learn in college, learning to cook in marriage, and learning to cope in motherhood. But the yearning tugged at my consciousness as I cleaned house, folded diapers, listened to sermons, took notes at PTA, cheered the Little Leaguers, and made small talk at women's teas. Sometime, somewhere, I knew I would arrive at a place of *being*, when all the accumulated experience of my years would come together and I would feel wise and finished.

Somewhere in my forties I began to panic. It hadn't happened yet, and I was haunted by the fear it might never happen. I could see the years flipping past like pages in a book, a book that had an end. I wanted some sense of existential worth before the last page was turned.

And all that time, while I was looking for the answer in maturity, age, and "oldness," it was waiting for me in the very surprising niche of "newness." A rather odd Victorian philosopher helped me find that niche and gave the object of my search a name—my Ideal.

Thomas Carlyle was a Calvinist who had disavowed his faith in his youth and then returned to his own revised edition of it when he was older. He wrote about this spiritual pilgrimage in *Sartor Resartus*, beginning with "The Everlasting No," in which he described the evil, negative forces that had attempted to suppress him. From there he passed through the "Centre of Indifference" and arrived triumphantly in the kingdom of "The Everlasting Yea."

I was amused by Carlyle's startling rhetoric and unorthodox theology, but I found some link to my own quest in his quaint ramblings, especially in these words:

> Here or nowhere is thy Ideal: work it out therefrom; and working, believe, live, be free. Fool! the Ideal is in thyself, the impediment too is in thyself: thy condition is but the stuff thou art to shape that same Ideal out of. . . . the thing thou seekest is already with thee, "here or nowhere," couldst thou only see![1]

It wasn't original, of course. I could name a dozen others who had unveiled that eternal truth, among them Jesus of Nazareth. But somehow Carlyle's noisy voice awoke me, and I began to understand at last something about being new.

I was still digesting this challenge to find my Ideal in the newness of the present while we were vacationing at our cabin on a Minnesota lake. Inspired by a neighbor's enthusiasm over the lake at sunrise, I decided to get up one day and see it for myself.

I sat on the dock, holding myself to keep out the chill, watching the deep rose glow spread behind the smudge of shoreline across the lake. Ripples on the water caught the subtle glow, tossing it back and forth on the corrugated surface. Soon a crimson light touched the whole morning, bathing it in a soft blush—and me along with it. The sky turned from rose to blazing orange; then, in an instant, to brilliant gold. The sun heaved itself over the horizon and was lifted lightly upward, like a balloon

off its string. It was a splendid, golden moment in which
I felt a part of creation and beginnings.

As the sun rose higher, the world turned pale and
light, and I could see details on the opposite shore. I
usually saw that side of the lake in a blur of green and
brown in the afternoon light, as if I were looking through
a dark glass. But now I was seeing face to face not only the
cabins and trees across the lake, but the eternal, creative
possibilities of the moment, of every moment of my life.

Those cabins and trees across the lake had always been
there in living, detailed color. Each day waves lapped the
golden shore and boats bobbed on the undulating water.
They were the same each morning, noon, and evening.
But the light was different in the morning newness.

That morning brought a different light for me, too—
one that could change the way I saw my opportunities in
what Carlyle called "the poor, despicable Actual." I didn't
have to wait for *being* on the other side of some future
rainbow. I could become new, not only on days when I rose
early to greet the sun, but whenever I chose to *arise*—"to
come into being." My Ideal was "here or nowhere," in
the newness of each day, as a born-again daughter of the
One who creates all days and all beginnings.

> But it is with [our] Soul as it was with Nature: the
> beginning of Creation is—Light. Till the eye have
> vision, the whole members are in bonds. Divine
> moment, when over the tempest-tost Soul, as once
> over the wild-weltering Chaos, it is spoken: Let
> there be Light![2]
>
> —Thomas Carlyle

Paul M. Schrock

Not by might, nor by power,
    but by my Spirit, says the Lord of hosts.

—Zechariah 4:6, <small>RSV</small>

Here Is
Power

As I began looking around my own Actual, doubt hovered like a cloud over my newly enlightened self. What power did I have to call forth that light into all my days? It was one thing to watch the sun rise over the lake; it was quite another to make it rise over a day filled with piles of dirty clothes to wash, meetings to attend, quarrels to settle, and meals to cook. I wasn't sure I could bring that golden touch to my tinplate days—until I remembered the men and women who followed Jesus.

Of all the people who ever looked around at their own "poor, despicable Actual" and wondered how it could be turned around, the disciples must have been among the most bewildered. Here were people who had walked away from their jobs and their homes, risking all on a poor Galilean preacher who had just been executed as a criminal. Their own safety was in jeopardy, and what little money they had saved had gone with the treasurer of the band to his own unsavory grave. Things had not turned out at all as they expected. They were powerlessness personified.

And yet, in a few weeks, they were out on the roads again—not as followers, but as leaders. They were still without money or employment. They were still being watched by the authorities. The established church wanted no more to do with them than when Jesus was alive, but things had changed. The Pentecost experience had brought power to carry out the mission their Lord had left with them. It was not the authority they had asked for—to sit in glory at his right hand—but power of a different sort, the kind spoken of in the Book of Zechariah, the kind Jesus had promised when he said they would be "armed with the power from above" (Luke 24:49). They had moved out of the valley to the mountaintop.

Or had they? I wondered about this as we were driving through the wild expanses of Wyoming and Nevada. We often found ourselves traveling in what seemed to be a flat plain or deep valley, then were surprised to see elevation signs that indicated we were really up on a mountain. Our reasoning was based on what we saw around us, visual impressions that prevented our realizing how far we were above sea level. The disciples must have felt the same way—everything around them spoke of failure and rejection, of tumbling into the gaping jaws of a hostile canyon, when, in truth, they were on a high plateau.

This power was also quite different from the kind they had exercised on a trial run when the Master was still with them. They had returned from that first discipling experience bursting with pride. "In your name, Lord," they said, "even the devils submit to us" (Luke 10:17). Later, sobered by their temporary power failure at the time of Jesus' arrest and crucifixion, this ragtag army spent a time of prayerful preparation before becoming agents in the unleashing of a power greater than they could imagine, a power so compelling they could not "possibly give up speaking of things [they had] seen and heard" (Acts 4:20), even when it meant their imprisonment or death.

During that time, the disciples learned to play the game with new rules. The rules they thought were operating—power over people exercised through the governing strength of kings and rulers—were turned upside down by the One who had entered their lives three years before. "You have heard it said . . . but I say unto you . . ." became a litany of unlearning the old ways and an introduction to a new kind of power.

In her study of what gives people power to bring well-being into their lives, Gail Sheehy points out the best time to take risks is when one is the most scared. "People with the best chance of sustaining well-being," she says, "are those willing to let go of it."[1] When the disciples discovered their own courage lacking, when they were ready to run for cover, a residue of Presence allowed them to set aside the urge to retreat and compelled them instead to reach for risk. They found that the peace given them by the Master was not a sitting-with-hands-folded rest, but a sense of direction and destiny, moving them to "obey God rather than men" (Acts 5:30).

On my way through the "me decade" of the 1970s, I explored some of the advertised avenues to personal power, from assertiveness training to transactional analysis, from prayer groups to positive thinking. Each had its patterns, paradigms, and promises. I tried visualizing myself as an assured, assertive person in complete control of all possible situations. I tried to follow the models I read about or saw around me, but somehow I always fell short. I had a mental picture of what I thought made up wholeness—a serene, unsinkable saint whose life had been stitched together with no stray threads escaping from the seams, a life of harmony unbroken by discord. Shouldn't my goal be that kind of wholeness, in every aspect of my life, in order to show God's power at work in me?

That was one of those questions that never got answered while I was asking it. Then one day I read a trivial book in which all the well-ordered people behaved in perfectly reasonable, well-adjusted ways. In addition to being dull, those people and their lives were entirely insignificant. That was certainly not the kind of wholeness I wanted. I thought of men like Thomas à Becket, Abraham Lincoln, and Martin Luther King, Jr.; of women like Florence Nightingale, Harriet Tubman, and Mother Teresa; of the men and women who followed Jesus. These people were driven by a Force that compelled them toward their destiny despite the tumult that resulted in their lives. I began to understand another dimension of Augustine's restlessness that found rest in God. It was not a rest that shut the world out, but one that let the world in to "find your strength in the Lord, in his mighty power" (Eph. 6:10). I began to sense some of that rest when I stopped trying so hard to generate the power to be whole.

That goal, I realized, was serving the god of myself. If I am ready NOW to give up trying to fit into this society's mold and to accept being out of joint with a world that is in disharmony with its Creator, then I may be ready to use the power I received in baptism, the vast "resources of his power open to us who trust in him" (Eph. 1:19).

Does this mean I will never fail? Hardly. God does not promise to make me a spiritual heroine, to say nothing of a paragon of personal achievement. The followers of Jesus went after him into martyrdom and exile. Their names are not recorded with the potentates of history, but because they were willing to bring the power given to them into their Actual, using the only tools they had— their memories to recall, their feet to travel, and their tongues to tell—I have available to me the good news that brings power to all people.

> We are no better than pots of earthenware to contain this treasure, and this proves that such transcendent power does not come from us, but is God's alone.
>
> —2 Corinthians 4:7

H. Armstrong Roberts

For wisdom will sink into your mind,
and knowledge will be your heart's
delight.

—Proverbs 2:10

Here Is Wisdom

I have not been frugal in my hopes for gifts from God. I have wanted them all—love, patience, joy, longsuffering, self-control—I could not think of one I could do without. But above all the rest, the one I most hoped for was wisdom.

I wanted knowledge, of course, so that I could answer all the questions my children asked me and so that I could pass any test with ease. But I wanted more than facts and book-knowledge. I wanted that kind of wisdom that sits brooding, with chin in hand, KNOWING. I wanted understanding and discernment with which to counsel others and guide my own paths. I wasn't sure how to go about attaining this virtue; I think I assumed it would come almost naturally, along with gray hairs and a double chin, the result of much living and learning.

A friend and I once discussed what worried us about getting old. We were young enough at the time not to think of old as doddering senility. Old to us was "grown up," a time when we were supposed to be in control of ourselves and our environment. I confessed I was afraid I would never learn to be comfortable wearing hose all the time the way my mother and her friends did. My friend said she feared she would not be able to unfurl a cloth across the dining room table the way she had watched her grandmother do it. We agreed those manifestations of maturity would be signs we were really grown up and ready to take our places in the world.

Gradually, I began to yearn for more substantive symbols of knowledgeable adulthood. When I was in high school, I learned to identify a few symphonies and concertos, and I read all of A. J. Cronin's books—my idea then of the road to culture. In college I studied French, music, and art, with a little economics thrown in to round out the practical side. I continued my private education between diapering and feeding with the discovery of Brother Lawrence, Thomas a Kempis, and C. S. Lewis. I was learning, my mind was being stretched, but was I becoming wise? Would I ever become wise?

Early on, I accepted the proverbial counsel that wisdom began with the fear of the Lord. I knew I must look to the Author-Creator for what I was seeking, but I began to realize that, even with divine assistance, that kind of wisdom might not arrive automatically, like a Social Security check, when I reached a certain age. I read and prayed and studied, hoping that someday it would all come together and I would, at last, receive the mantle of wisdom. The writer of Ecclesiasticus claimed, "To all mankind he has given her [Wisdom] in some measure . . ." (1:13), and I was patiently awaiting my share. I didn't really expect it to happen before I was old and experienced. "First the blade, then the ear, then full-grown corn in the ear . . . ," Jesus had said (Mark 4:28), so I was willing to wait.

My entry into the kingdom of NOW called that think-ing into question. Could it be that wisdom was available even to those without credentials, to those who had not served a long apprenticeship or read a thousand books? I began poking into corners of cobwebbed thought, and before I knew it, I was looking with corrected vision at the people around me.

My children: Perhaps I was not set on this earth solely to rescue my children from their follies. Perhaps they were sent, in part, to rescue me from my assumption that I always knew more than they—what to do, how to do it, and when not to do it. Perhaps I could listen and watch and learn from them—openness, spontaneous joy, unquestioning love. Perhaps I would find wisdom in their questions more often than in my answers.

My husband: Perhaps I could relinquish my attempts to catch up to what he had learned and be willing to learn from him. I did not relish the idea of scrambling for crumbs from the master's table (Wisdom in the Bible is, after all, feminine), but I could accept some select mor-sels from his plate of extraordinary common sense and be willing to acknowledge his portion of insight from the Spirit, who makes no distinction between male and female.

My parents: Perhaps I could learn from my parents'

virtues and integrity as well as from their mistakes.
Perhaps their unassuming practice of Christian generosity and unconditional love could be a signpost to the
place where wisdom could be found.

My friends: Perhaps if I stopped trying to prove my own
worth and wisdom to those around me, I could hear their
inner voices that speak in an enduring language. Perhaps
I could look for some form of wisdom in everyone I meet
and affirm the sightings and soundings of sapience in the
sea of every soul.

Even with such a cloud of witnesses around me, I
found that as my awareness grew, more questions than
answers appeared. My intellect was awed by great philosophical problems that loomed like mountains around
my dwelling place. My emotions were stirred by suffering
and grief that twisted and knotted lives like chains in a
drawer. My soul was puzzled by the ways of a God who
came to earth as an infant and chose fishermen and tax
collectors to carry on his work. I didn't want easy
answers, but I longed for some satisfying interpretation of
life's eternal issues.

Gradually, long before I read the lines, I began taking
the advice attributed to Rainer Maria Rilke to be patient
with all that's unsettled in your heart and learn to love
the questions themselves. Answers became less important as I probed and pondered the questions and became
comfortable with paradox. I learned to think more like
the Hebrew, to whom "a seemingly completed action is
never truly completed in the . . . mind and imagination,
but still lives and moves in the present, and that those

imperishable Realities which make his present will continue to make his future as well."[1]

I had to object when I heard a sincere young man tell a study group that the Bible had an answer to every question, as if it were an almanac of pat solutions to life's most complex problems. "No, no! The Bible has answers, but not look-it-up, put-your-finger-on-it kind of answers! It has answers of knowing and believing and becoming, not referenced resolutions to every problem you pose."

Answers may come when God brings this mad world back to himself. Meanwhile, we are called to be obedient to whatever knowing God has given us. Madeleine L'Engle wrote, "One does not have to understand to be obedient. Instead of understanding—that intellectual understanding which we are so fond of—there is a feeling of rightness, of knowing, knowing things which we are not yet able to understand."[2] In faith, then, I can wrestle with the mystery in my Actual, seeking wisdom in every here and now.

> The spirit of awareness is one that receives, waits, seeks, and asks. To quest and to question is a way into the real.[3]
>
> —Herb F. Brokering

W. L. Hazelwood

I am here! O my God.
I am here, I am here!
You draw me away from earth,
and I climb to You
in a passion of shrilling,
to the dot in heaven
where, for an instant, You crucify me.
When will you keep me forever?
Must You always let me fall
back to the furrow's dip,
a poor bird of clay?
Oh, at least
let my exultant nothingness
soar to the glory of Your mercy,
in the same hope,
until death.[1]

—Carmen Bernos De Gasztold

Chapter Four ――――――――――――――――――

Here Is Hope

Years ago I came across a strange phrase in the Book of Zechariah—"prisoners of hope" (see 9:12 RSV). The oracle speaks of rescue and restoration of those who have been enslaved. I found it odd to think of being *imprisoned* by hope, which is more often thought of as the agent that liberates us from the bondage of present stress. Like the reader who told Madeleine L'Engle she had read *A Wrinkle in Time* when she was younger and "didn't understand it, but I knew what it was about,"[2] I wasn't sure I understood how one could be a prisoner of hope, but I knew what the passage meant.

Some years later, when I shared an anxious year with people whose husbands and sons were listed as POW or MIA following the war in Vietnam, I began to understand. Those people clutched a desperate hope that kept them imprisoned in the kingdom of uncertainty. Those individuals who had given up hope were free to live their lives apart from it. They could bury their loved ones in their hearts and begin living without them. For those persons who hoped, however, all life revolved around "when" and "if." They could not escape the prison of hoping their family member would return. They attended to the duties of daily living. They grew older, and their children grew up. Life went on in them and around them, but they remained, as Annie Dillard says, "caught holding one end of a love" . . . reeling out "love's long line alone, stripped like a live wire loosing its sparks to a cloud, like a live wire loosed in space to longing and grief everlasting."[3]

Hope came to an end for many of those families when their loved ones were not among the prisoners returned. A few still cling to that hope in spite of overwhelming evidence that no more American servicemen remain alive in Southeast Asia. For them, hope is no longer expectation, but merely a means of clinging to their confidence in the strength of survival.

Some of those people claimed an added dimension to their hope, the kind Paul speaks of that does not disappoint or mock us "because God's love has flooded our inmost heart through the Holy Spirit he has given us" (Rom. 5:5). The hope we have in Christ differs from all other expectation because it is a sure thing.

That difference is what brings hope into the NOW. Although our hope is, as Paul says, laid up for us in heaven, it is there now, and we don't have to wait to leave this earth to collect all its benefits.

That was good news to me as I navigated the passage into middle age. Sometimes I felt as if I were being put on hold while, as *The Rubáiyát of Omar Khayyám* puts it, "The Wine of Life keeps oozing drop by drop, the Leaves of Life keep falling one by one."[4] I knew the Creator was shaping me for something, but I was more impatient for an end to my period of preparation than a child waiting for Christmas. My journal during that time reads like a roller coaster ride: "The writing I've been doing seems dull; nothing seems to work . . . I can endure because of the strong certainty I have that whatever happens I am not alone, that I can lay all my misgivings, my failures and my inadequacies at God's feet as worthy sacrifices." Yet the theme of "God in me" sustained me, its melody weaving a pattern of hope from my strains of doubt and discouragement.

The writer to the Hebrews speaks of "seizing" and "grasping" the hope set before us, the hope that is here now for us to take. "It is like an anchor for our lives, an anchor safe and sure" (Heb. 6:19). That anchor keeps me steady when the winds of discontent beat at my moorings, an ever-living hope that frees me from the fetters of the past and opens me to every opportunity of the future.

In *Black Elk Speaks*, the aging Indian describes a vision he had when he was nine years old. He was transported from his dwelling to a place beyond earth where he was shown images and symbols of what had been and what was yet to come. There he "saw more than I can tell and I understood more than I saw."[5] The vision left him with a feeling of presence and power, so that even when he went back to being a boy not yet old enough to hunt the bison, his vision set him apart from the community. It was a vision of expectation, for he knew he was destined to act out the drama he had witnessed. Nevertheless, it was also a vision of hope that enriched his life each day as he grew up. It awakened him to relationships in nature and humankind. It gave meaning to his existence and to his activities. He had been chosen.

When Lucy says good-bye to Aslan, the great lion who portrays the Christ figure in C. S. Lewis's *Voyage of the Dawn Treader,* he tells her they shall meet again soon. "Please, Aslan, what do you call *soon?*" The lion answers, "I call all times soon."[6] Hope is "all times," not just "when," not only "someday." The Lord of life has chosen his people. Those persons who answer God's call are freed from empty expectations to a hope that makes every day a due season.

> God dug his seed
> into dry dark earth.
> After a pushing up
> in hopeful birth
> and healing bloom
> and garland grace
> he buried it again
> in a darker place.
>
> Twice rudely-planted seed,
> root, rise in me
> and grow your green again,
> your fruited tree.[7]
>
> —Luci Shaw

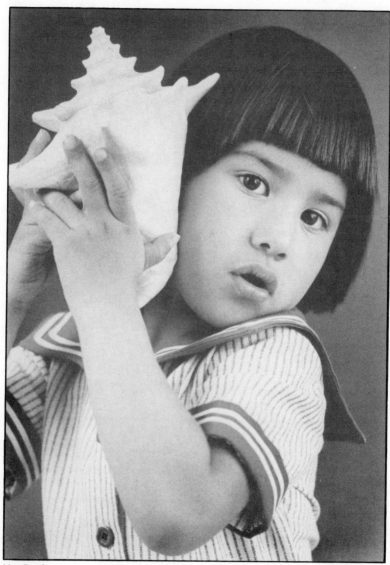

Mimi Forsyth

God does not die on the day when we
cease to believe in a personal deity,
but we die on the day when our lives
cease to be illumined by the steady
radiance, renewed daily, of a wonder,
the source of which is beyond all
reason.[1]

—Dag Hammarskjöld

Here Is
Wonder

Wonder took on a new meaning for us this year as we welcomed our first grandchild into the family. There was, of course, anticipation (Would it be a boy or girl? Would the birth coincide with two nearby family birthdays? Who would he/she look like?), anxiety (Will the birth process go well? Will the baby be "all right"?), and, of course, excitement (We are going to be grandparents, uncles, and great-grandparents!). But when we saw the miracle that was Tracy and held her in our arms, there was only wonder.

In her we found recollection of our own newborn sons, perhaps some subconscious remembrance of our infancy, and most certainly, the renewed wonder of creation itself. As I studied her face and looked into the eyes that looked back so unflinchingly into mine, I sensed a bonding that went beyond the intellectual knowledge that some of my own genes had a part in her formation. "I know her," I told her mother. We were, from the beginning, part of each other.

Is this what bragging grandparents struggle to express when they pass around pictures and describe the unique wonder of their once-removed offspring? Trying to explain the wonder I feel is like trying to explain blossoming—the explosion of feeling can only be expressed in terms I have learned and others can understand: "She is beautiful; she is responsive; she is aware." Later on, it will be: "She is intelligent; she is loving; she is achieving." I must find words to capture the wonder, lest it escape.

In some cultures, naming something has great significance. To know someone's name is to have control over that person. In the second account of creation in Genesis, God gives Adam the privilege and responsibility of naming the creatures. In the first account, the ones made in God's image are given dominion over the earth and all its inhabitants. Are those acts two faces of the same coin? However I may qualify an answer, I must admit there is some mystery connected to naming, and the question then arises: "If I name (or describe) something, have I diminished it?"

As a communicator, I feel a need to describe things, to name them with just the right words. I think there are at least two schools of thought on whether or not this enhances experience. In my school, where the teacher is a stern disciplinarian who goes by the rules and believes in a thorough exploration of every subject, the dictum says taking time to describe something in specific lan-

guage makes me more aware of that something's essential
qualities. The other school, where the headmaster wears
flowing robes and thinks a long time before he speaks,
claims words inhibit experience.

Perhaps that second school is saying what Sam Keen
says in *Apology for Wonder*, that "wonder adds nothing to
our knowledge *about* an object. It is rather that the object
comes into focus and is respected and relished in its
otherness."[2] Wonder, then, is not the intellectual curi-
osity of an adult mind, however that mind might marvel
at its findings. Wonder is—perhaps, for I am only trying
to name something that may be unnameable—a child-
like "oh!" that comes on us unbidden and unannounced.
Like Fourth of July firecrackers spraying a sprinkling of
stars across an inky sky, it brings bursts of joy into our
dark nights.

I remember many such nights, when we sat on
blankets with other watchers, trying to anticipate where
the next burst would appear. But part of the wonder was
the surprise, the not-knowing-where-to-look. Sometimes
we thought we could anticipate a special one, but often
that turned out to be a disappointing flash and dismal
fizzle. The very best, most wonder-full ones were those
that streaked silently to the top of the sky, then showered
a brilliant canopy of stars over our heads. All of us were
children at those times, caught in a spell of wonder.

Fortunately for us, those displays were calculated to
last only as long as we were able to sustain our sense of
awe. (Don't ask me how this is determined; perhaps it
was all based on economics—how much they could

afford to buy.) My senses can absorb only so much wonder, then I enter the realm of jadedness, where no miracle can touch me. On the other side of that world is the
kingdom of the routine, where my sensitivity to any kind
of marvel is dulled by habitual uniformity.

Wonder, then, is at home with HERE and NOW.
When I look back on wonder, it is reflection; when I look
forward to it, it is anticipation. Only in the present is it
wonder, as Keen says, giving new meaning to an event or
object, involving me in the mystery and the presence of a
gift unsought. "Let them be what they are in their own
right," he says, lest by attempting to shape them into
more acceptable forms, we lose them. Jesus called people
to this wonder of otherness—in faith and religious living, in values and judgments, in sight and perception.

When I think of this kind of wonder, I remember what
Mark Twain said about the Bible, that it was not the
parts he didn't understand that bothered him, but the
parts he understood only too well. Sometimes the NOW
wonders of God revealed are too strong for me, like the
sight of Moses coming out of the tent where he met the
Lord God. Then I would prefer reflecting on the wonders
of the past, where they were directed at someone else, or
of the future, where they will be another's responsibility.
Wonders are unmanageable and unpredictable. They
shake my mountain of knowing with their mysteries.

Above all, however, wonder proves to me I do not have
a God I can wrap up in a neat theological package tied
with doctrinal ribbons. Every time I think I have God's
nature defined or described, my Creator bursts out of the

lines I have drawn and shows me an unexpected wonder I cannot explain. Why, for example, would a God who orders the ants into uniform marching squadrons and directs the plants to exchange the toxic air around them into life-giving oxygen also create the sun that, at the same time, dries my clothes and draws moisture from the ocean to make rain? Why should a God whose voice called a universe into being come to me as a helpless infant, a powerless prophet, and a murdered martyr?

The wonders are here, all around me, every day. Perhaps I should take a cue from Alice in Wonderland and discover at least one wonder-full thing each day. On the other hand, if I am open enough and quiet enough, I may not even need to look. Perhaps wonder will find me.

> For:
> A creative spring that bursts through the barren
>   winter,
> implosions of hope and explosions of joy,
> a new chance each morning,
> and sometimes—
> heaven now.
> Thanks, Lord.[3]
>
> —Marilee Zdenek

C. L. Tucker

Does the road wind uphill all the way?
    Yes, to the very end.
Will the day's journey take the whole long day?
    From morn to night, my friend.

But is there for the night a resting place?
    A roof for when the slow dark hours begin.
May not the darkness hide it from my face?
    You cannot miss that inn.[1]

—Christina Rossetti

Chapter Six

Here Is Contentment

It has not been easy for me to learn the lesson of contentment in the NOW. In fact, I am still rehearsing that theme, quite often playing the wrong notes and having to go back and study the score. Paul's "I have learned, in whatever state I am, to be content" (Phil. 4:11, RSV) is easier preached than practiced.

When we bought a horse for our son in Arizona, we were told the animal had "personality." We discovered that meant he was not blessed with the state of contentment. If Flash did not choose to be ridden the day we chose to ride, he would toss his head and reach back to bite at the stirrup. When he chose to lunch in a neighboring stall, he would work the lock off his gate and roam the stable yard until he found a menu that suited his taste. Flash had plenty food and water of his own, but the hay always appeared tastier on the other side of his fence.

As aggravating as it was to get bills for his gourmet tasting sprees and for blankets he chewed up just because

they were there, I could identify with old Flash's
instincts. Wasn't the house someone else bought a much
better buy than ours? Wouldn't it be nice to live somewhere that wasn't so hot in the summer? Won't it be a
relief to move away from here and get out from under all
those responsibilities I have become involved in? There
are always those times when my mind wanders from my
Actual to some emerald field on the other side of my
boundaries.

I indulged in those escapist fantasies more often than
usual one year when I taught a ninth-grade Sunday
school class. I had taught younger junior highs for years
and learned to love that exciting—if sometimes exas-
perating—growing time. But this class was different.
The students were just enough older to be, in their
minds, beyond the kid stuff of Sunday school. They were
there because it was required as part of their confirmation
study. I was teaching a decidedly captive audience.

I thought the year would never end. Each week I
prayed and prepared myself and my lessons, trying every
innovative trick I knew to capture their imagination.
Each week I arrived with a positive confidence, and each
week my expectancy was shattered with rudeness and
indifference. Although those hours put a strain on my
contentment quotient, I clung to the thought that those
students were, in spite of themselves, kids of the Kingdom and if God could love them, God could help me love
them, too.

Gradually that began to happen. Behavior and attention were no better at the Sunday morning sessions, and I

didn't turn into a whiz-bang charismatic teacher. Most of
the time it was just a matter of getting through the hour,
but I could sense in myself an increasing awareness of
feeling for the students, a feeling that was not of my own
making. The class showed no evidence of such
awareness, however, and when it came time to say our
good-byes on the last Sunday, contentment still escaped
me. Relief was not enough. I was glad to have it over, but
what had I accomplished?

For one thing, as I looked back on the year, I had
grown in my understanding of unrequited Christian love.
The struggle and frustration I felt drove me to look
beyond my own skills and knowledge to the Giver of all
perfect gifts. I had to go past the teacher's guide and
teacher training programs to the Teacher. I found myself
reading the scriptures in a new way—seeing not the
successes of the prophets and Jesus, but the ways in
which they had failed by any normal measure of accomplishment. If I couldn't quite proclaim my contentment
in the words of Paul, I could at least share my discomfort
with the prophets, who were "reproached and mocked all
the time" (Jer. 20:8). I found it true, as Abraham
Heschel said, "To be a prophet is both a distinction and
an affliction." [2]

This tale does not have a storybook ending, but a
postscript scribbled on the last day of class brought it to
completion. The one young man who had troubled me
most with his disruptive behavior, the one I had the
hardest time learning to accept as a lovable child of God,
hung back to say good-bye. No apology, no thanks, no

turnaround behavior, but the gesture itself was all of those to me. It put contentment in perspective.

In his poem "Journey of the Magi," T. S. Eliot describes the rigors of traveling at "just the worst time of the year . . . and such a long journey" through the eyes of one who had made the trip. Seeking shelter, finding towns unfriendly, dirty, and expensive, the members of the caravan traveled in a state of discontent, longing for the summer palaces, sherbets, and silken girls they had left behind. Nevertheless, after witnessing the nativity, a birth that was "hard and bitter agony for us, like Death, our death," they returned to their places, changed enough by the experience to feel ill at ease in the "old dispensation, with an alien people clutching their gods." In reflection, the aging wise man concluded, "I should be glad of another death."[3]

Perhaps that is a part of the concept of being "buried with Christ." I must bury my alien gods of contentment (the state in which the rosebush has no thorns and the river runs without rapids) in order to be resurrected into the kingdom of contentment, where birth and death dwell together, where I can complain and praise without being contradictory, where my peace comes, not from insurance against aggravation, but from the assurance of "God with me."

> The good road and the road of difficulties
> you have made to cross; and where they
> cross, that place is holy.[4]

Paul M. Schrock

Anywhere he went he found he was always
somewhere. He could not get away from
everything.[1]

—Herb F. Brokering

Here Is
Home

In the years we have traveled with the air force, I have been grateful for biblical admonitions to welcome the sojourner. In each place where we lived, hospitable Christians have welcomed us into environments of homelikeness. Even before the dishes were unpacked and we had learned the way to the grocery store, we were enveloped in the warm nest of the Christian community.

It didn't take an "aha" experience to teach me that home is where I am—or it had better be if I want to enjoy living. One of the mixed blessings of the transient life is that the lack of rooting and long-term belonging creates a certain flexibility. People on the move have a realistic understanding of how little it takes to live well. Most of us have been called upon, at one time or another, to live without furniture and familiar belongings or to live with the things that were supposed to go into storage. Some of us have been squeezed into crowded,

inadequate dwellings or dumped into a cavernous house
we could not hope to furnish completely. We have been
moved from the tropics to frigid northern plains, from
the edge of a sprawling metropolis to a lonely desert
outpost. And we know, if we are wise, that we must make
home wherever we are, at whatever price, and we must
make it quickly.

We do not have the luxury of long-range planning to
decide how to drape the windows or landscape the yard.
If we are to enjoy our new home at all, we must do those
things when we first arrive. Like the preacher who said,
"I would rather do something and do it wrong than do
nothing at all," we must risk buying the wrong house or
putting the children in the wrong schools each time we
move. We decide, then go about living with our decisions to make that place home.

Most of the people we meet create that kind of home
wherever they find themselves, but there are a few who
never seem to manage to find home anywhere. For them,
the last place they lived is always the best, their present
assignment always the worst. Because they have no home
inside themselves, they can never be at home in the
world around them.

That sense of home, of belonging, probably begins in
childhood. In the early days of our marriage, our parents'
homes were still more "home" to us than was our newly
established household. When we went back to visit in
those homes, we relaxed into a familiar pattern of being
cared for. There we found reminders of our time of
belonging—pictures we remembered from our child-

hood, the milk pitcher that had faithfully filled cereal bowls and coffee cups, the desk with its cubbyholes full of pens and pencils, letters and photographs. Our attic apartment, even with its worn carpet and almost-antique furnishings, could not provide the same sense of identity. It was more like a training ground where we were still taking the polish off the newness of our union; there were no memories to make it home.

Gradually our own dwelling place, wherever it was, became home to us. Familiar objects that moved from place to place, our own developing family history, a growing maturity that increased our independence—all of these combined like twigs and scraps of yarn to build our own secure nest. Our concept of home grew from "Home is the place where, when you have to go there,/ They have to take you in"[2] to "Home is where we can be ourselves, where we can grow together or alone, where we know hospice and belonging."

Jesus did not have such a home after he left the carpenter's shop in Nazareth. "Foxes have their holes, the birds their roosts; but the Son of Man has nowhere to lay his head" (Matt. 8:20). Nevertheless, Jesus was, more than any of us, at home in every place, in each situation. As master of the Sabbath, he needed no rules to govern his conduct; as friend to those of high and low estate, he was welcomed into the homes of others; as servant of all, his behavior was "right and meet" for every situation. In spite of his out-of-stepness with the prevailing society in which he lived, he was at home because he brought "home" to everyone he met. Joann Haugerud has trans-

lated John 14:23 to read: "If you love me, you will keep
my word, and God will love you and we will come to you
and make our home with you."[3]

In one of Moses' many arguments with the Lord God,
he spoke of this quality of presence that makes a difference in our Actual. Yahweh had renewed his promise
to deliver the land of Canaan into the hands of his
people, but he refused to accompany them any farther on
their journey for fear he would destroy them in his anger
at their stubbornness. The people were only just recover-
ing from their revels before the altar of a god of their own
making. The taste of its burnt remains clung bitterly on
their lips. In spite of their backsliding, Moses felt compelled to defend them.

"You have told me to lead this expedition. You told me
I was chosen especially for the job—the right man, you
said. Now if that is the case, please tell me what to do
next. These are *your own people*. If you don't go with us,
don't bother to send us at all, for how can anyone know
we belong to you unless you are with us? How else shall
we be distinct from all the peoples of the earth?" (Exod.
32:12–17, AP).

This, then, is the other dimension of finding home
wherever I am—this distinctness, this practice of the
presence of God, my eternal Home, in house or office,
field or factory, school or shop. It has, in the long run,
nothing to do with the walls around me or familiar things
or geographical setting. It has everything to do with what
Gerhard Frost calls "Homing in the Presence."[4] The
Presence is what makes the difference, transforming the

most humble and inhospitable surroundings into a wel-
coming refuge where no one is excluded, where all can
be "at home."

> A child in a foul stable,
> Where the beasts feed and foam;
> Only where He was homeless,
> Are you and I at home;
> . . . .
> To an open house in the evening
> Home shall men come,
> To an older place than Eden
> And a taller town than Rome.
> To the end of the way of the wandering star,
> To the things that cannot be and that are,
> To the place where God was homeless
> And all men are at home.[5]

> —G. K. Chesterton

Therefore do not be anxious about tomorrow,
for tomorrow will be anxious for itself.
Let the day's own trouble
be sufficient for the day.

—Matthew 6:34, RSV

Here Is
Faith

The word *faith*, like the word *love*, has evolved a myriad of mystical meanings. It has developed, at the same time, a cliché quality that reduces it to something near meaninglessness. Faith can refer to a person's religious persuasion (she is of the Catholic faith), or it can be the topic of a popular song ("I Believe"). We speak of "great faith" and "weak faith" and "no faith at all." Most of all, however, we think of faith as being about something that will happen in the future.

The scriptures burst with examples of this kind of faith. What but faith could have called Abraham from his comfortable homeland to a new and uncertain country? What but faith could have brought Moses back from his exile to the palaces of Pharaoh or urged Noah to build an ark on dry land? Faith held the prophets firm against ridicule and persecution. The promises of faith summoned the Israelites out of Egypt and brought Jacob to a small-town well to find his wife.

There is a segment of this concept of faith (in itself too deep and wide to fathom in a lifetime) that does point ahead. "Wait on God" it counsels the impatient ones; "hold on" it whispers to the suffering ones. Another segment of faith looks back to what has gone before. Celebrating the Passover event from year to year, century to century, confirms the acts of God on behalf of the chosen people. Looking back to see the hand of God working in my life verifies (makes true) my faith in God's power and willingness to act in me again.

But there is a NOWness to faith that I began to search for as I was awakened to the experience of newness. I wondered if I must always wait for God to act (I was one of the impatient ones). Even when I reached the place where I was ready to accept a promise and wait for it, I was still left with an empty cup until that promise was fulfilled. *This life that is sliding by like transparencies flitting across a screen must be made up of more than waiting,* I thought. What about NOW?

Although I was older than most of them, I found myself in sympathy with wives who had their career wings clipped every time their husbands were transferred. School teachers, accountants, department store buyers—they all began at the bottom again with each move—and sometimes there was not room even at the bottom. I had just begun to have some opportunities in publishing when we moved to Spain. That move represented a dream come true; it was an assignment we had hoped for and were delighted to receive. My *work, enhanced by the experience of living in a country so rich in history and art, can certainly continue by mail,* I thought.

I found, however, that my new zip code all but cut me off from former contacts. In the United States, where so much work depended on the telephone, communication by mail across an ocean was apparently an anachronism. I had, it seemed, disappeared off the U.S. coastline.

I am not sure now why I cared so much then. There was certainly enough to do without the interference of writing deadlines. Our children were convinced we visited every castle and cathedral in Spain. There were other cities and villages to explore, histories to learn, a language to master. In addition, I was plunged into the frantic round of activities an American community overseas develops to keep its members from being bored and lonely.

In spite of finding each day too short for what I already had to do, I lived with a sense of being "on hold." I often saw my days from the viewpoint of the writer of Ecclesiastes, as "emptiness and chasing the wind" (Eccl. 1:14). At one point, after a long spell of busyness—visits from family and friends, conferences, meetings, and projects—I wrote in my journal that I felt caught up in a flow, a current that was pulling me along apart from any will of my own. I questioned whether living that way was my delusion or my destiny.

It was easy at that time to look toward the day when we would move back to the States and I could begin over, when I could map out a life to my liking and begin doing "real things." I was waiting with relish for my overdue season.

It wasn't Thomas Carlyle that called me back to the present this time, but I was gently reminded through other knowing or unknowing servants of the all-wise One that "real things" might be close at hand. Long ago, I had discovered the philosophy of Brother Lawrence in *The Practice of the Presence of God.* In preparing a workshop one day, I came across some notes I had made on an old translation of his work: "Not greater things for God, but next things." I read this to mean not future things, but things at hand. As a person who had spent nearly as many hours in kitchens as the good friar, I could identify with "next things," those things that never completely disappeared when a task was done, but merely waited around to be done again. The more I pondered these words, the more willing I was to do "next things" during those years in Spain. Sometimes I considered those things important, such as heading a project to raise money for an orphanage. Sometimes I realized they were as simple as being at home when a friend needed to talk or meeting someone's mother at the airport. Whatever they were, I was more willing to see them as my faith calling for the moment.

I was called back to this truth often as I became immersed in the "next things" of daily living, along with the joys of travel and learning. Looking back, I can see it as a wonderful time of filling-up far more than pouring-out. And I can agree with C. S. Lewis who, his biographer Kay Lindskoog says, confessed ". . . we make the error of resenting as interruptions to our chosen life-work the obligations that are actually set for us." She goes on to explain: "It seems as if Lewis was often set to the humble task of helping individuals who hurt; his *chosen* life work was teaching and writing about things he felt and believed."[1]

But I was receiving more help than I was giving. As I read my journal notations from that time, I realize how much learning happened through my reading and meditation, all of it clearing highways across my desert, lifting up my valleys, bringing low the mountains, and smoothing out the rugged places, laying foundations for things to come. The door into the kingdom, as C. S. Lewis said in *Voyage of the Dawn Treader*, was from my own world.[2] Even in my discontent and impatience, I was being helped to exercise faith—in next things as well as future things, in the NOW as well as in the time to come.

> We are not among those who shrink back
> and are lost; we have the faith to make
> life our own.
> —Hebrews 10:39

Mimi Forsyth

If you want a religion
to make you feel really comfortable,
I certainly don't recommend Christianity.[1]

—C. S. Lewis

Chapter Nine ─────────────────────

Here Is
Truth

C. S. Lewis resolved his battle with the discomfort of Christianity by describing it and explaining it,
by putting all the stray wisps of doctrine into an orderly,
methodical pattern. He called it *Mere Christianity.*

That book and its approach to the faith were more
than helpful to me at a time when my mind was being
awakened to ideas that tore holes in the safety net I had
woven around my beliefs. Lewis was so logical and made
so much sense. I couldn't imagine how anyone could
remain an unbeliever after an encounter with Lewis's lucid
thinking. But of course they did. I remember giving *Mere
Christianity* to a seeking friend, confident it would answer
all her questions. It did not. The arguments made no
sense to her at all, and I couldn't understand why. I felt
like Jesus talking to the Pharisees: "If I tell you what is
true, why don't you believe me?"

I wanted her to see the whole truth and nothing but
the truth as I saw it. I didn't understand then what I have

been learning ever since, that truth is not some isolated absolute that exists for its own sake. And that it is revealed sparingly, measured to our own needs. Gerhard Frost explains that God "is too kind to drown us in all the knowledge we crave. He doesn't give more than we can hold; sometimes we must wait to be made larger cups."[2]

In the Old Testament, God simply said, "I am." To the people who had been conditioned by Greek philosophical thinking, Jesus said, "I am the truth." Even that was not enough for Governor Pilate who pressed Jesus further—"What is truth?" He didn't wait for an answer. Perhaps he knew he would get no more than a question in return, or a puzzling Hebrew paradox, when what he wanted was a plain answer that would simplify his task of acting as judge in that bothersome foreign outpost. He wanted truth to be as simple as telling who cut down the cherry tree or how to tell black from white. The Jews, he knew from experience, would try to tell him black and white exist together—even though they might not be able to explain what every artist knows today, that neither is a true color. One (black) is the result of a surface absorbing all the light rays that strike it, and the other (white) occurs when a surface reflects all the light rays. The truth about color, in fact, is that no object has color in itself. Without the reflection of light, there would be no color.

Truth itself is nearly as elusive, unwilling to be caught in any doctrine designed to contain it. Truth sweeps as wide and deep as the minds of the world's greatest thinkers; it dances in the first fleeting glimpse of understanding that begins to unlock the mysteries of thought in a child. Truth hides in the mysteries of the universe and reveals itself in the undisguised glory of each sunrise.

The ancient Hebrews were wise enough to recognize and accept what to our minds seems inconsistent—that God could be at once hidden and revealed, the Lord could be a God of both fear and love, of joy and judg-ment. Their heroes were not cardboard models of merit, but full-bodied participants in the drama of life. They had as many vices as virtues, as many weaknesses as strengths. If Moses and David were to appear together on a talk show today, they would probably argue over points of the Law and its interpretation. They might find fault with each other's style of leadership and personal way of living. They might describe truth in different languages and carry different banners.

What they could agree on would be the reality of their God in the life of their people. Does God become man-ifest in a burning bush and a fiery mountain or in the accuracy of a slingshot and an anointing in a farmyard? It did not matter. Their God was the one God of Israel who had created the world and all that is in it. Truth was all around them. Truth was inside them and in the Creator "whose every *what*," Gerhard Frost explains, "counters every *why*."[3]

During the time our sons were growing up, I was called as an arbitrator to many a scene of battle. Each boy told his side, the truth as he saw it. Sometimes there was a truth to be discerned—yes, one boy did hit the other first—but more often there were two "truths"—an intricate series of events that left both boys in an equal state of guilt. Then we had to negotiate. With children that can take a long time, because no one wants to give in or admit someone else might be even a little bit right and he or she might be even slightly wrong.

Adults, even Christian adults, continue to fight the same battles. My version of the gospel is holier than yours. My church speaks more truth than yours. My way of living is more Christian than yours. Once I have defined truth and drawn my own boundaries around it, I am secure, not only in my own "rightness," but in everyone else's "wrongness." In fact, the more wrongs I can find in others, the more secure I am about my own rights.

A wise retreat leader once told a group that his list of non-negotiables grew shorter as he grew older. He had given up fighting over theologies and practices that were not central to his faith in Jesus as Lord. Although there were undoubtedly many people in his denomination who thought he was going soft and losing his faith, he contended his faith was stronger than ever because he had turned his attention, as the Hebrews did, to the One who is truth in its fullest sense, as it was and always had been.

Mary Ellen Chase says the language of the Old Testament "deals in empty spaces." Certainly God could have provided the chosen people with a complete, annotated, official directory of truth that would have prevented all this searching. Instead God gave one simple statement ("The Lord is . . . one Lord, and you must love the Lord your God with all your heart and soul and strength" [Deut. 6:5]) and one not-so-simple commandment

("Love your neighbour . . . like yourself" [Lev.19:18]). All the additions to those basic truths proved to be more hindrances than help. By the time Jesus came, the people were so entangled in rules and arguments over truth ("Who sinned, this man or his parents?" "Whose wife will she be?" "Is it lawful to heal on the Sabbath?") that he could only call them back to God's first revelation, to the One in whom all things come together.

"Love God above all, love yourself and your neighbor as yourself"—if I don't hear that behind all the philosophical rhetoric and theological argument around me, I have lost my grasp on the only truth God really cares if I understand. If my life is not a witness to that command, even the most simple statement of faith is excessive. I would rather have rules and truth spelled out in so many specific formulas, but I must accept instead a generic, no-frills truth. It is not comfortable, only true.

> I am the LORD, there is no other.
> I do not speak in secret, in realms of darkness,
> I do not say to the sons of Jacob,
>   "Look for me in the empty void."
> I the LORD speak what is right,
>   declare what is just.
>   —Isaiah 45:18–19

W. L. Hazelwood

Out of the dark into light
The people were created for beauty,
The head, the mind
To think beauty,
The eyes to see beauty,
The ears to hear beauty,
The heart to bear love towards all.

—Creation Chant of Tao Indians

Here Is
Beauty

I was going to call this chapter "Here is Poetry," but I was afraid it would sound too lofty and esoteric. Everyone can relate to beauty, but many people feel no affinity for poetry. Perhaps those people do not venture beyond the dictionary definition, which says simply "the writing of poems." The thesaurus draws just as narrow a circle around the word despite its multiple listing of poetic terms: *rhyme, verse, ballad, jingle, quatrain, tercet,* and *hexapody,* to name a few.

Nevertheless, poetry and beauty might be considered almost synonymous. Poetry, the highest and most eloquent of literary forms (even the best prose follows poetic style in precision and imagery), mirrors and articulates the beauty we experience, whether on the grand scale of panoramic vistas or in the minuscule drop of dew on a rose petal. In addition to describing the beauty that meets the eye, poetry gives expression to the width and breadth and depth of emotion in the human heart.

When familiar language fails us, poetry parts the curtain to reveal the truth hidden behind the words we know so well.

But poetry is more than words; it is rhythm and style and emotion; it is history, music, mythology, and art, pulsing the heartbeat of humankind in primitive tribes and sophisticated societies alike. It is art in all its forms, whenever that art is true and pure.

Beauty and poetry often get put aside—like Sunday clothes and the best bottle of wine—for special occasions. Beauty is seeing the Grand Canyon on our vacation or going out to the opera for a rare dose of self-improving culture. There are a few serendipity experiences, of course—the brilliance of a golden sunset, the velvet softness of a perfect rose, the lingering balm of a poignant melody. But on the whole, we do not go about expecting to meet beauty very often in our day's activities.

During the years when I was immersed in motherhood, from the daily nurturing chores to all the accompanying demands on time and talents, I took only occasional excursions out of my labyrinth of routine tasks into the ordered realm of loftier things. *Someday,* I promised myself, *I will devote more time to the pursuit of beauty.* Someday, I was certain, the house would echo with the sound of great symphonies instead of silly squabbles. One day it would be safe to surround ourselves with objets d'art to inspire daily aesthetic encounters. And above all, our library would be full of books dedicated to bringing beauty and poetry into our lives. We would sit, each in a chair before the fire, sipping sherry from etched crystal glasses while a Bach fugue played on the stereo, reading a leather-bound volume of something deeply significant.

I am not sure I have let go of that dream altogether— it is a pleasant, if somewhat irrelevant and irrational, vision. But that dream now is only a tributary of the great river of poetic experience I find—if I look—in my poor, despicable Actual days. When God fixed "the earth on its foundation" (Psalm 104:5) and "spread out the heavens like a tent/and on their waters laid the beams of [his] pavilion" (Psalm 104:2–3), he expressed himself as the essence of beauty far beyond the grasp of my poor finite mind. God created it all "very good," and he created me in his image so that I could respond to every wonder of beauty his mind made visible.

I love the graphic Old Testament descriptions of creation. Those writers do not wallow in abstractions, but give me images of the Power and Imagination that "made the moon to measure the year" (Psalm 104:19) and "gathered the sea like water in a goatskin" (Psalm 33:7). They speak of a God who "gauged the waters in the palm of his hand . . . with its span set limits to the heavens . . . held all the soil of earth in a bushel . . . weighed the mountains on a balance and the hills on a pair of scales" (Isa. 40:12).

God's human creatures lost that primitive response to beauty when they attempted to cage it and shape it into manageable categories. Definition surely must be the archenemy of art. When we attempt to define, we confine. We put "art" into museums and symphony halls and university libraries and congratulate ourselves on our aesthetic achievements. We endow critics with the authority to decide for us what we should appreciate and what we should ignore, declining nature's invitation to the banquet of beauty prepared for us each day.

When our family traveled the back roads of Spain, we often saw a shepherd sitting on a hillside, miles from any community, "keeping watch over the sheep." I wondered what he thought about, day upon monotonous day. I knew his sphere of experience was painfully limited. He probably had become a shepherd when he was very young and, once committed to that calling, was more or less cut off from any kind of community life.

About the time I was pitying that poor man's plight, I remembered the psalm writers whose majestic lyrics always move me more than other verses. *Perhaps,* I thought, *those shepherds on the lonely, barren hills have sharper eyes to see and keener ears to hear than most of us who take our culture in measured doses, like dutiful patients swallowing a tonic.*

Gerhard Frost agrees: "The stuff of life is made of personal relationships, the repeated and common experiences of *this day*" where God "provides us, his children, with daily situations which contain within them the highest and the best."[1] That means I can look for the "very good" God made in every encounter, in any surrounding, and at any time. God's beauty was spilled out upon the earth for all to enjoy.

That is easier for me to say now, here in a hilltop

setting of woods fanned by light sea breezes, where flowers brighten paths and doorways and birds soar against the azure sky. It was quite a different story when I was confined to a sterile office with no windows, shackled with responsibility for work that was never finished, but only repeated itself in weekly cycles. Where was the beauty there? What kind of poetry lives for those who labor in smoky factories, for waitresses with tired feet and crabby customers, for police officers working the vice squad, for persons whose eager spirits are imprisoned in unresponsive bodies?

During one of my earliest encounters with official culture, I discovered a piano concerto by Edvard Grieg. I responded to the whole work, which set my mind to roaming in mountain forests and deep fiords. There was one particular passage, however, a very short one, whose exquisite melody—like water spilling down a rocky glen—poured into my very depths like pain. Each time it comes, sweet and swift, and then it is gone. I wondered why that theme was not repeated; it was certainly worth hearing more than once. Then I wondered if it was so beautiful because it came only once, like Blake's "winged joy" or Tennyson's "short swallow flights of song, that dip/ Their wings in tears, and skim away."[2]

Wordsworth's answer to the absence of beauty in our lives was that "the world is too much with us; late and soon,/Getting and spending, we lay waste our powers:/ Little we see in Nature that is ours. . . ."[3] Perhaps it is true that in my life in the fast lane of asphalt territory I take no time to notice nature's small wonders. Perhaps, too, I think beauty can occur only in such wonders or in the ripened fruit of great artists. Perhaps, on the other hand, I can learn to look for beauty in the ordinary, like those people who create art out of discarded junk. Madeleine L'Engle says, "Art does not reproduce the visible. Rather, it makes visible." I can, then, find beauty in the arch of a bridge, the curve of a cheek, the angle of a shadow. It may appear, then, in a warm smile across a noisy room, a mother's lullaby on a crowded bus, or the furrowed faces of those who have lived life deeply. Perhaps I will not have to strive to find beauty after all, but simply let it come to me—here or nowhere.

> Lord,
> if
> Your creation is still unfolding,
> and You are still releasing the power
> of Your might,
> then
> put me in love
> with the fountains that break out of nowhere,
> deep hidden rivers,
> silent seas under deserts,
> and magnify the wonder and wishing
> of unfolding inside myself.[4]
>
> —Herb F. Brokering

Mimi Forsyth

Sometimes we are prisoners in prisons of our own design. We've carefully built our walls; we've made our prison safe and comfortable and then we have chosen to lock ourselves inside. And we do not call it a prison at all, we call it our home or work or responsibility. We are very careful to post guards so that nothing threatens the security of our prison. Some of us live and die there and suppose that we have been happy and that living was good.[1]

—Molly Dee Rundle

Here Is
Freedom

How many people in this land of the free and the brave have a sense of that freedom? How many are brave enough to claim it? How many of us prefer life in our prisons?

While I am on temporary parole this summer from what I sometimes consider my prison, I have been trying to examine the walls of that confinement and how they got there. I am looking at my present sense of "here or nowhere" freedom and wondering how I can retain that when I go back to my real, despicable Actual. We came to this place of learning, my husband and I, he to study, I to work. We brought only the necessities and are living within the restrictions of what we can cook with three pans and what we can wear out of two suitcases. Outside of his classes and a few optional activities, our time is our own to schedule. We have no television or telephone, no meetings or social obligations. We are free from the expectations and responsibilities that bind us at home.

Nevertheless, we are not totally without accountabil-
ity. He has books to read and papers to write. I have a
deadline to meet. We have bills to pay and contacts to
keep with family and friends. We get up early and go to
bed late and probably spend less time in frivolous activity
than we do at home. Why, then, do I find myself many
times a day taking a deep breath and stretching my arms
wide in a conscious celebration of freedom?

My first step in finding an answer must be in deciding
what imprisons me at home. What expectations and
demands smother my autonomy, my ability to be in
charge of my own days and hours?

Necessities claim a major portion, of course—the
work day, getting to and from, caring for the home,
doing all the things that "have to be done." But each
time I am forced to live as simply as we are doing here,
whether it is by choice on a camping or cabin vacation or
as required when we move and wait for our household
goods to arrive, I wonder what I really *need* to live
comfortably and how many of my conveniences are actually burdens that make life more complex. Which are the
essentials that contribute to my well-being and which
only add more requirements of maintenance and care,
eating away at my already too-few hours?

Each time we move, we discard boxes and bags of
"stuff" we find we can live without. Sometimes the storage areas of our homes dictate what we keep and what we
give away. I seldom feel a loss when those things leave;
more often I am overjoyed with the space their departure
creates. It is breathing room, territory in which to

expand. Perhaps I *can* live with less in order to gain that space.

I have always had great problems with time. There will never be enough time to carry out all my grand designs. There will not even be enough time to indulge all my inclinations toward simple pastimes. I don't think I want to change that. I think I want my reach always to exceed my grasp. Somehow, though, I want to be able to do *some* of those things within the time I have left from the necessaries. As I look in perspective at my life at home, I realize how much of my time is spent in things I simply fall into—a short shopping trip that draws out to three hours; a small duty that grows because I don't know when to say no; too many tasks extended by the distraction of television; too many things done or done in a certain way because I have always done them or always done them in that way. Perhaps I can budget my time more carefully to use each hour more productively, whether that be in activity or rest and reflection. And perhaps I should not try to do *everything*.

Trying to do everything, I have concluded, is the tap root of my problem that needs to be dug from the depths where it has been anchored for far too many years. My "Messiah complex" may stem from a desire to prove I am as capable and saintly as anyone else who is going about doing good, or it may be my response to all the "you shoulds" I have heard throughout my life. I have only recently learned to sit and enjoy certain events without feeling I should be in the kitchen or in some way helping.

I have yet to join an organization in which I have not felt compelled to "do my part." I live with chronic attacks of guilt for all the friends I have not visited, all the letters I have not written, all the books I have not read, all the money I have not given, all the generous gestures I have withheld. I am not saying I want to give up caring or serving. I am simply trying to learn to make more conscious, careful decisions about what I do, acknowledging that I cannot do it all and that I will miss some fine moments of life by putting some things aside. On the other hand, perhaps the moments I invest with care may reflect the luster of the pearl of very special value, value enough to pay the price.

But is that freedom? Isn't freedom denouncing restraint and plans, letting go and riding the winds wherever they carry us? That is certainly the answer coming from certain voices in our society, but I am listening to others to find my answers. Yesterday a friend was describing the eagle's life cycle and habits. That powerful ruler of the air, he said, sometimes waits for hours for just the right current of air to carry it soaring to the loftiest heights of the sky. In order to catch that current, it must disregard all the good winds that blow by its perch. The eagle is free to choose; it uses its freedom to choose the best.

In "Studies in Words," C. S. Lewis describes the emphasis Aristotle placed on the concept of freedom. Free persons, he says, as opposed to those who are slaves, are called upon to pattern their lives after the order of the universe, with a responsibility to be all they can be.

Slaves of that time, Lewis says, randomly used what little time of freedom they were allowed, with little regard for its value. The Greek word for freedom—*eleutheros*—was used more often to describe an ethical quality than legal status, he explains. Free persons were expected to behave in a special way—with generosity and justice. In contrast, literature of ancient times shows the dominant characteristics of the slaves were not abject servility, but cunning and shrewdness, a looking-out-for-Number-One mentality.

This idea casts a new light on the words of Jesus: "You shall know the truth, and the truth will set you free" (John 8:32). We know from other discourses that Jesus advocated generous love and living in God's kingdom. It all fits! He was not pushing a let-it-all-hang-out philosophy, but one in which the cost is calculated before the direction is chosen. We are, as someone has pointed out, not only "free from" but "free to." I am cut loose from the chains binding me to my self-centered interests, freed to choose the house with many dwelling places prepared for me, where I am free to grow and learn and be all that I can be.

Real freedom—the kind that Jesus promises—is not a guaranteed ticket to a smooth-sailing cruise or a ride on a road without potholes. Real freedom usually means swimming upstream, against popular currents. Sometimes I wish that were not so, that I could relax and let the swift stream carry me. But then I would not be free; I would be subject to its rushing or meandering, to both waterfalls and swamps. My freedom lies instead with the

One who can bring *eleutheros* into everything I do—here
or nowhere.

> Freedom is not enough. Freedom that is its own goal
> has no design, but is only an impulse . . . a stolen
> fox hidden against our hearts.[2]
>   —Margaret Mead

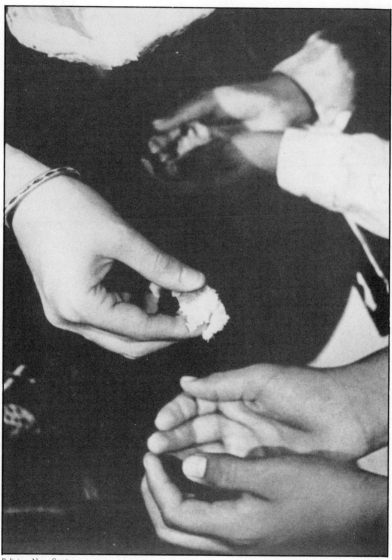

We are God's handiwork,
    created in Christ Jesus
    to devote ourselves
    to the good deeds
    for which God has designed us.

—Ephesians 2:10

Here Is
Servanthood

The concept of servanthood that was a popular theme among the country's theologians for a few years never quite caught on in the pew. For one thing, the shadow of suffering, servanthood's companion concept in the writings of the prophets, never could be blown away completely by the breezes of exalted rhetoric. A society bent on looking out for Number One is not much interested in servanthood, much less suffering. Its people, whether in the church or out of it, might acknowledge that some persons have to be servants and some have to suffer, but volunteering for either is out of the question.

Jesus is fairly clear on this point: "Among you, whoever wants to be great must be your servant, and whoever wants to be first must be the willing slave of all—like the Son of Man; he did not come to be served, but to serve, and to give up his life as a ransom for many" (Matt. 20:27–28). He did give his life—in the villages and countryside of Galilee and Judea; in teaching and healing and in washing feet; and finally, on a lonely hill outside Jerusalem. Like the preacher in the pulpit, he told us what he was going to do, he did it, and he told us afterward what he had done. It should be clear, but the question still eats at us: How, then, shall we be servants?

That question began nibbling at my complacency about the time I was looking back at the twenty years I had spent doing things in the name of motherhood and volunteerism. A lot of things were coming together at that time. Feminism was moving into religion—or maybe it was the other way around. At any rate, while women in the church were beginning to look at traditional dogmas and practices with eyes enlightened by consciousness raising, I was getting ready to turn in my apron and retire from the business of being "servant of all." I wasn't planning to resume a career I had set aside for marriage or to carve a place for myself in the corporate structure. I had no career to resume and no goals under which to prop my ladder of ambition. I just wanted to be someone other than the chaplain's wife or Mark's mother or the Tuesday Red Cross lady or Karl's den mother or the seventh-grade Sunday school teacher. I believed I had fulfilled my servanthood. I was ready to begin fulfilling myself.

As I ventured out of the world of the familiar into new territories of learning, however, I could not give up serving altogether. I continued to care for my family—although a little less obsessively. I kept working in the church and the schools—although a little less often. Whether it was from a sense of oughtness or willingness,

I cannot say. Doing such things had become a pattern in my life, tasks I performed almost without question.

But I did begin to question them as my learning and working load increased. From part-time school to part-time job, to full-time school to full-time job—the time and energy I had to give in service kept shrinking. Soon I found myself in a position where the work load grew like bread dough in a warm room, expanding and spilling over into hours meant to be spent outside the office. The person inside me who could never say no to a good cause was stung with guilt every time I didn't sign up for a committee. *Someday*, I thought, *I will get a job that will allow me some serving time on the side.*

But because I was trying to learn to live in the land of NOW, I wondered if there could be a way to serve where I was, in my Actual of fifty-five-hour work weeks. And I wondered if there wasn't more to being a servant than doing things, a dimension beyond noblesse oblige. When I began my search with a New Testament concordance, I discovered the Bible uses several different words that are all translated "servant" in English. The one Jesus used often was *diakonos*, from which our word "deacon" derives. These are the passages that contrast greatness and servanthood, that call us to a special relationship in the kingdom, where one doesn't pull rank but lives under the grace of mutual submission. This word denotes ministry, being set aside for a special purpose.

The word used to indicate household servants or slaves is *doulos*. Jesus uses this word in the parables about masters and servants. A number of the apostles use this term in describing their relationship to Christ, who invited them also to be his friends: "I call you servants no longer. . . . I have called you friends" (John 15:15). In him, the disciples found the freedom to serve as partners in ministry.

I was struck by some exceptions to the apparent patterns as I looked at the way these words were used. Although *doulos* was always used for a household servant or slave, John uses *diakonos* in the story of the wedding at Cana (see John 2:1–11). I puzzled over this usage and could only conclude that, although the servants were performing what appeared to be a routine duty, doing it in obedience to Jesus transformed that duty into an act of ministry. They were partakers in something greater than themselves. In the story of Mary and Martha (see Luke 10:38–42), the word *diakonos* was used also—it was not mere cooking and serving that was being done, it was ministry to the Master. Again, the women who were healed by Jesus and rose to serve him (see Matt. 8:14–15) were acting as *diakonos*, ministering in acts of grateful love.

Brother Lawrence, a monastery cook who took his job as an act of penance because he had a natural "great aversion" to the kitchen, wrote that God outwitted him and brought him out of the slavery of penance into servanthood. "Having accustomed myself to do everything there for the love of God, and with prayer upon all occasions for the grace to do his work well, I have found everything easy during the fifteen years I have been employed there."[1]

Beulah Laursen described lay servanthood as including serving a client "in a just and productive way," having to do with the "Christian dimension of on-the-job behavior; with the moral and ethical decisions of any trade or profession; with the way one sees oneself in relation to God, neighbor, nature, and the structures of society."[2]

I began then to look for ways of serving where I was, as a *diakonos*. Could I be more patient with an employee or complaining caller? Could I stop to listen when I would rather be busy about something else? Could I speak the truth in love when it was necessary? Could I perform my work with as much honesty and truth as I knew how? And could I do it all in the name of One who has called me friend?

I found myself struggling, as W. H. Auden says of Dag Hammarskjold, to unite the life of activity to the life of contemplation.[3] Like Robert Frost, I wanted my avocation and my vocation to merge into one calling.

> But yield who will to their separation
> My object in living is to unite
> My avocation and my vocation
> As my two eyes make one in sight.
> Only where love and need are one,
> And the work is play for mortal stakes,
> Is the deed ever really done
> For Heaven and the future's sakes.[4]
>   —Robert Frost

Sallie India Linebaugh

Satisfaction is a lowly thing;
how pure a thing is joy.[1]

—Marianne Moore

Here Is
Joy

An awareness of the difference between satisfaction and joy dawned in my awakening mind about the time I realized the world, like Gaul, was divided into three parts: the good, the bad, and the in-between. Somehow I had grown up in almost total ignorance of the latter. I can remember seeing the film based on Arthur Miller's play *All My Sons* and being bewildered because I didn't know which characters to hate and which to cheer for. The father, who had betrayed his integrity, was a cheerful, good-hearted man who loved his family. His son, who I supposed was the hero of the play, was not strong enough to send his father to jail or to forgive him. In my childhood books, and even in those books I had read from the adult shelves, the lines between heroes and villains were clearly drawn, and there was no mistaking one for the other.

I soon realized that I had been trying to see life that way by putting people into categories of good or bad, making everyone fit into the well-defined squares and circles I had drawn with my prejudiced pen. I still fight that—mentally dismissing people I meet as certain types before I give them a chance to show me who they really are. I have come close to missing out on some fine relationships and some valuable learning experiences by hesitating to look beyond their surface appearance. It wasn't easy to break out of the checkerboard world of black and white where I always knew which side the players were on, however.

So when I thought about satisfaction and joy, I decided, of course, in favor of the pure, clear trumpet sounds of joy. Let someone else settle for the stolid, monotonous tones of satisfaction. I didn't want to clomp through life in sensible shoes; I wanted to dance in slippers that lifted me above the ordinary to ecstasies unknown. It wasn't difficult to choose one over the other. What was hard was making it stick.

It is one thing to say, "I choose joy," and quite another to live it in the Actual of final exams, broken romances, spoiled dinners, morning sickness, whining babies, quarreling siblings, and budget balancing. After a few stabs at finding joy hiding between the six A.M. feeding and the last glass of water at bedtime, I began to wonder if I had misjudged satisfaction. Maybe, I reasoned, I could get by on that until the day I was safely removed from the dailiness of homemaking and ready to be swept into the intoxicating realm of "better things." I didn't know exactly what those things might be, only that they surely would be waiting on the other side of my rainbow to drench me in joy.

Satisfaction was a cozy companion. I snuggled into its soft cushions, warmed my feet by its fire, and sipped its mellow wine. Life was good in comfortable homes where growing boys played football on the lawn and friends shared meals at our table. In between daily chores, there was time for camping trips and sewing lessons, for symphony concerts and Bible study. After bills and taxes, there was money for an occasional meal out and a new couch for the living room. The One who satisfies the earth with the fruit of his work had apparently satisfied us, his children, with every good thing.

When the thunder clap sounded in my peaceful valley of satisfaction, I didn't know it was heralding the end of an era in my life. The days of satisfaction were waning, the days of joy yet to come. First I had to move through the netherworld of insecurity. When my husband left for a year of duty on a remote island off the shores of Alaska, he left behind five sons, a house, a car, a dog, a cat, and a very frightened wife. During my years in the school of marriage, motherhood, and volunteerism, I had earned A's in following, but I hadn't even signed up for the course in leading.

Satisfaction took on new meaning. At first, just getting through the day without a catastrophe filled me with gratitude. I was satisfied just to have a few moments to myself before I fell asleep at the end of a day. I didn't ask for much in my prayers at those times—simply to be equal to the responsibility I faced each day. But the Parent who gives better gifts than the children of the family can ever ask for was nudging me out of the nest I had built in the broad branches of satisfaction.

Only later would I understand what was happening. Walter Starcke explains it this way: "No creativity takes place when there is a total security because a secure thing is immovable and unchangeable. I cannot leave this piece of wood secure and carve a statue out of it at the same time. I cannot leave the eggs in their shells and bake a cake with them. There must be an element of insecurity in order to create, to be what we call alive." [2]

My coming alive meant that I not only came through the experience, but came through it stronger. I had learned from Brother Lawrence "the greater perfection a soul aspires to, the more dependent it is upon grace." [3] The greater my need, the larger the measure of grace. When the year was finished, the shards of satisfaction lay broken at my feet, shattered by the pure, sharp tones of joy in one who made my "morning and evening sing aloud in triumph" (Psalm 65:8).

That is not to say that I still don't have trouble getting out of bed in the morning, that I never wrestle with discouragement and despair, or that I don't find enduring satisfaction in what God has given me. How to describe the difference when joy arrives to live inside? Jesus said he would bring "life . . . in all its fullness" (John 10:10).

Fullness is rising, dancing, singing—falling, stumbling, weeping—and rising to dance and sing again. That to me is joy and life in all its fullness. Joy is not—to me, at least—a cloud-nine address. I have found, as Robert Frost once wrote, "Now no joy but lacks salt,/That is not dashed with pain/And weariness and fault."[4] Such joy is a stirring, a moving, a changing.

I have spent many reflective evening hours on the dock at our lakeside cabin, watching and feeling the mood of the day. Some evenings are peaceful and quiet, a balm for the restless spirit that needs to be still and wait. At other times, a recent storm leaves traces of turbulence that send the waves lapping urgently against the shore, as if to win back the sand and rock they have deposited there. Then things are in flux, creating a feeling of excitement and expectancy. One such day, when motorboats were kept tied to piers where they bounced drunkenly on wind-whipped waves, I saw a sailboat skimming the water in the middle of the lake. Its journey across the lake was not inhibited by the wind that kept other vessels off the water. Rather, the gusts filled its sails with life and power.

On a day when I recorded joy in the realization of a long-awaited hope, I compared it to the joy I felt during the long waiting, praying time. *Two sides of the same coin,* I said to myself, *both gifts from the same loving Lord.* New joys are affirmed in those places in me that were made strong by God's presence during the times when "anxious thoughts filled my heart." Then and now, I will proclaim with the psalmist, "When I felt that my foot was slip-

ping,/thy Love, O LORD, held me up. . . . thy presence
is my joy and my consolation" (Psalm 94:18–19).

> A laugh, a cry, the business of the world . . .
> And my whole soul revolves, the cup runs over,
> The world and life's too big to pass for a dream.[5]

—Robert Browning

Bruce Partain

One who knows sorrow
For a long or little while
Learns a new language.[1]

—Jean Fox Holland

Here Is
Grief

I have no right to attempt any kind of commentary on the subject of grief. It has touched my life only through the lives of those individuals with whom I have shared some anguished moments. That would be reason enough to leave it out. Add to that my determination to bring a positive perspective into my NOW, and I could almost justify leaving this task to someone who has walked through deeper valleys. Almost.

Perhaps just because this is one required course of life where I cannot claim experience, I have been drawn to try to understand it. For it is the one experience we cannot choose. It comes unbidden, often falling like a "sudden, swift sword" to carve deep, gaping wounds that threaten our wholeness. Its visit cannot be postponed to a more convenient time or place. It should not be locked away in a secret attic and ignored. Like an uninvited guest, grief comes unbidden, to be reluctantly admitted or refused entrance to the inner spaces of being. The wise host will manage to wring some meaning from the visit, but that will not make the stay any less painful.

We were overseas when we received word that the son of close friends had been killed in an automobile acci-dent. Although I could have done nothing to ease their sense of loss had I been with them, the distance between us seemed to magnify my feeling of impotence. Later, when Paul's mother and I spent an afternoon together, she relived the experience with me, a generous act of sharing that enabled me to participate in their grief. This same generosity had allowed John and Maggie to find meaning in their suffering. They had begun a sharing group for others in their community who had met the dread dragons of grief, and together they had found a measure of healing.

To each of those persons they touched, they gave the gift of faith active in the NOW. Maggie recounted the dreadful moments after the phone call. Later, when the impact of the news began to take hold, Maggie would admit she felt that she could go "screaming down the street in utter madness." But at first, she and John stood alone in quiet, fearful awareness that this tragedy would mark their lives forever.

"We looked at each other and decided that if there was anything at all to this faith we had been professing, we had to claim it NOW, and stand on its promises."

The siren had gone off. This is NOT a test. This is the real thing. Because they are persons of great sensitivity who do not settle for paint-by-number pictures of life, they probed the depths of their grief and their faith.

Perhaps they suffered more because of it, but through the process they moved beyond the pain to find not answers, but meaning.

Abraham Heschel, in commenting on the role of the prophet in society, says, "More excruciating than the experience of suffering is the agony of sensing no meaning in suffering."[2] That is not to say that Paul died in order for his parents to become more alive; it is to say his parents could take what was and ever shall be a tragic loss and let it lead them beyond despair to a fuller experience of grace. Meaning is, as Eugenia Price says, *"encountered . . .not created.* Meaning is already there because God is there."[3]

God was there for Maggie and John in their suffering because the One was already there in their lives and because they chose to ratify that presence and its power to provide meaning. Without that, life is only breathing in and out. Ernest Hemingway once said life had meaning for him only as long as he could write, make love, and hunt. When illness deprived him of his ability to continue those pursuits, he ended the life that had ceased to have significance for him without achievement and accomplishment. He could find meaning only in what had been given, not in what had been taken away.

For some people who suffer debilitating illness or crippling infirmity, the physical suffering is insignificant compared with the loss of ability to do things that give their life meaning. My husband's grandmother kept her one-hundred-year-old mother busy hemming dishtowels because the pious woman could not bear to be "useless."

The hems were ripped out regularly to make more work for her gnarled fingers, along with a balm for her pining heart. This sense of futility often accompanies the closing years of life, when there seems to be no purpose in living, no more goals to aim for. After what they consider the most important statement of their lives has been written, many people simply sit back and wait for the period that will end the sentence.

Dona Hoffman found God in her suffering with cancer. She found God so real that she could argue with and joke with her Creator, as well as question or cry out to the One in her pain. Her willingness to invite God into her darkest journeys enabled her to encounter not a reason for her suffering, but meaning in it. She accepted the grace of Another who had not turned away from her pain. There, in her deepest valleys, she could say, "Yes, Lord."[4]

Someday I know I will be called upon to walk through one of those valleys. Will I be equal to the journey? How can I prepare for it? The only way I know is through the Way who said someone who can be trusted in little things can be trusted also in great ones. If I let him be a part of my ripples of sorrow and disappointment, he will be there when fiercer waves crash against the shores of my being. The Book of Job, a primer of suffering, offers no easy answers to the question we ask over and over again. The writer, very deliberately I believe, does not tell us why good people suffer, only that the Creator-God is a part of all that exists. The One who watched over the birth of the sea also attends the wild doe when she is in labor; the One who laid the foundations of the earth also sires the drops of dew and provides ravens with their quarry (see Job 38–39).

Like Job, I will ask no more questions. Like Job, I will stand in awe before the revelation that no purpose is beyond the Lord of life.

> To be touched by God is not to avoid suffering. It is to be drawn or driven into your authentic suffering, that suffering that is central to your own being and becoming, in the suffering of which you go limping in the daylight. [5]
>
> —Robert Raines

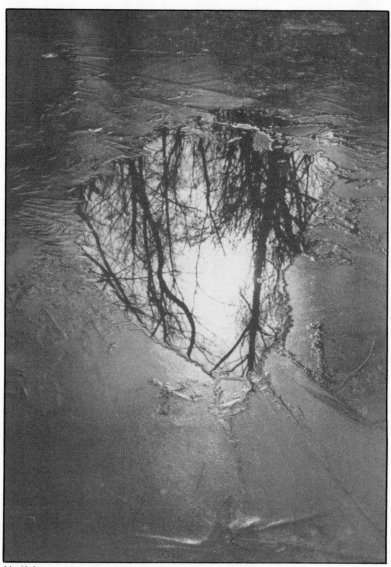

John Netherton

If I could fall into a black hole—
and magically look back over my shoulder—
I could watch the entire future of the universe
pass by. However, to someone standing outside
the black hole, unaffected by this gravity,
it would take an eternity for me to cross
the black hole's border. . . .[1]

—Rick Gore

Chapter Fifteen ————————————

Here Is
Eternity

Looking back to see the future, finding where we came from by looking at what we have become, holding eternity in an hour—suddenly poetry and science have come together. The knowing that poets could tell but not explain is now being described by scientists who explore the universe, its galaxies, stars, and solar masses. Albert Einstein defined time as a dimension, like up and down. Science now says space and time may exist on a continuum, interacting like two men riding alongside each other on motorcycles, throwing a ball back and forth.

For someone like me, whose mathematical skills are barely adequate for checkbook balancing, explanations of space and time continuums—even with motorcycle examples—are beyond comprehension. I have trouble getting past linear clock and calendar time. I think of space as what begins around me and extends to "out there." But I like listening to scientists talk about their new discoveries because it is like walking into the wild, imaginative world of fantasy writers. I can ponder forever the mystery of falling into a black hole and watching the future go by over my shoulder.

On another level, I am reminded of the infinite, surprising nature of the God humankind has been discovering at every turn of the telescope and focus of the microscope. Each time a Newton or Galileo or Einstein unlocks a secret door to "the way things are," there is another beyond it left to be opened. As our view of the dimensions of the universe expands beyond comprehension, we discover that what we thought was the smallest particle of matter is really made up of even smaller particles. From the infinitely vast to the infinitely microscopic, there seems to be no end to discovery.

Part of the wonder of our God, the "One who inhabits eternity" (Isa. 57:15, RSV), is that there is no end to that One's creation. Most scientists and theologians agree on this point—that creation is still going on. Science is learning something that theology has known for centuries—but has not always believed—that everything is connected in both space and time, so that creative happenings interact with each other, not only as they are present in the same space and time, but as they are present in the past and future, up there, down here, and out there. For example, the communication equipment aboard an early U.S. space flight picked up a radio program that had been broadcast in the 1930s. The light of a star that died long, long ago will reach us next year. A black hole, from which no light can escape, acts as a lens, bending rays to create a mirage so that an observer sees what is not there and doesn't see what is there. "What is unseen is eternal," says Paul to the Corinthians (see 2 Cor. 4:18, RSV), and what is eternal is what has happened, what is happening, and what will happen forevermore.

That is why C. S. Lewis could claim, as Kay Lindskoog says, "Since God is not in time, a Christian's prayer today is just as much present at the creation of the world as it is now or will be in the future. Prayers are in eternity with God."[2] Eternity didn't begin and will never end. Additionally, if Einstein's theory is correct, it never even rests to take a breath on its long journey to and from itself.

How can I comprehend such things? I cannot, and even those persons whose understanding goes far beyond mine cannot grasp the wholeness of it. They agree that the only things that are true are those things that are incomplete, and the only things they know are things that cannot be proven.

All of which seems to say that if eternity is, it is NOW. If God can make a difference in my life, that difference can come now. Memories of the past can be healed. I can look to an unending future in the company of the One who calls up the dawn and dwells in the frontiers of the morning. But I must call upon that same Power to bring abundant life to me in the present, here or nowhere.

The New Testament contains more than forty references to "eternal [or everlasting] life." The word *eternal* is seldom used without the word *life* added. They belong together, these two concepts from different families.

They have become one in a marriage of the physical and the metaphysical. Life and eternity, like space and time, are on a continuum, creating and interacting with each other.

The *National Geographic* issue (June 1983) that touches eternity in "The Once and Future Universe" includes a diverse slice of life as well. There are photographs of Cambridge students rowing on the placid Thames, of black-faced Kentucky coal miners, and of rare black-footed ferrets in Wyoming. Completing the issue is a story of divers who have recovered fifth-century bronze statues from the sea. Life—from galaxies light years away to the depths of this planet's oceans—is all a part of eternity along with me.

I cannot describe it or explain it; I can only think of simple symbols that remind me of the truth of eternity—like string art that crosses over and under itself in several dimensions, like these words that I am writing now but have been a part of me since I was "secretly kneaded into shape/and patterned in the depths of the earth" (Psalm 139:15).

While attending a conference in Berchtesgaden, West Germany, my husband and I took a Sunday afternoon walk past the busy outdoor cafes where carefree customers laughed and talked under bright umbrellas. We went up the hill where some ruined buildings hid among the brush, then hiked on to the top to enjoy a view of the surrounding mountains and picture-postcard valleys.

The next day I walked the same route with a guide who explained the layout of this place that had been

Hitler's notorious mountain retreat area. He pointed out foundations of buildings where war was plotted, fields where troops drilled for destruction, and craters, now covered with new grass, where bombs had fallen. It was too much to grasp—this place of tranquil beauty was once a giant, natural war room.

I came back again, alone, to let that past and my present mingle. The guide had said the hollows left by the bombs filled with water and he had gone swimming in them. Most of the buildings that were not destroyed by bombs were torn down or blown up, he said, because the people did not want to recall the infamy of that place. But they could not forget it, even with the buildings gone. And some, no doubt, still remember the thunder of bombs vibrating against the mountains, a sound that echoed in my mind in the quiet of the morning.

I walked back down the hill, over bunkers dug into the ground, back to the place where people now joined to praise the Prince of Peace. I walked on leaves of trees whose seeds were born in that wretched time past and whose own decomposition will nourish the life and growth of future vegetation. Eternity was happening where I was. "Remember where you stand," the writer to the Hebrews cautions, then adds, "Jesus Christ is the same yesterday, today, and for ever" (Heb. 13:8).

That means to me that no matter where I stand—in the midst of explosive destruction or in its silent after-math—I am a part of the eternal Presence that brings meaning to my yesterdays, todays, and forevers, here or nowhere.

God's eternity
breaks into time.
It is God,
I AM,
who was
is
and ever shall be
offering himself
to me
Here where I am
Now
when I am what I am.
Eternity
is
His majestic presence
given way to my insignificant
very present.
My hands cannot hold the abundance,
            the spilling over abundance
He offers me![3]

                              —Edna Hong

Notes

Preface
1. Henry David Thoreau, *Walden and Other Writings*, ed. Brooks Atkinson (New York: Random House, 1937), 297.

1. Here Is Newness
1. Thomas Carlyle, "Sartor Resartus" in *The Norton Anthology of English Literature*, ed. M. H. Abrams et al (New York: Norton, 1979), 2:997–8.
2. Thomas Carlyle, "Sartor Resartus," 998.

2. Here Is Power
1. Gail Sheehy, *Pathfinders* (New York: Morrow, 1981), 60.

3. Here Is Wisdom
1. Mary Ellen Chase, *Life and Language in the Old Testament* (New York: Norton, 1955), 35.
2. Madeleine L'Engle, *Walking on Water: Reflections on Faith and Art* (Wheaton, Ill.: Shaw, 1980), 22.
3. Herb F. Brokering, *Wholly Holy* (River Forest, Ill.: Lutheran Education Association, 1976), 33.

4. Here Is Hope
1. Carmen Bernos de Gasztold, "The Prayer of the Lark" in *Prayers from the Ark* (New York: Viking, 1962), 39.
2. Madeleine L'Engle, *Walking on Water*, 23.
3. Annie Dillard, *Holy the Firm* (New York: Harper & Row, 1977), 44.
4. *The Rubaiyat of Omar Khayyam*, trans. Edward Fitzgerald, in *The Norton Anthology*, 2:1218.
5. John Neihardt, *Black Elk Speaks* (New York: Washington Square Press, 1959), 36.
6. C. S. Lewis, *The Voyage of the Dawn Treader* (New York: Collier, 1970), 138.
7. Luci Shaw, "Seed" in *Listen to the Green* (Wheaton, Ill.: Shaw, 1971).

5. Here Is Wonder
1. Dag Hammarskjold, *Markings*, trans. Leif Sjoberg and W. H. Auden (New York: Knopf, 1964), 5.
2. Sam Keen, *Apology for Wonder* (New York: Harper & Row, 1969), 30.
3. Marilee Zdenek, *God Is a Verb!* (Waco: Word, 1974), 73.

6. Here Is Contentment
   1. Christina Rossetti, "Uphill" in *The Norton Anthology*, 2:1523.
   2. Abraham J. Heschel, *The Prophets* (New York: Harper & Row, 1962), 17–18.
   3. T. S. Eliot, "Journey of the Magi" in *The Norton Anthology*, 2:2283–4.
   4. John Neihardt, *Black Elk Speaks*, 323.
7. Here Is Home
   1. Herb F. Brokering, *Wholly Holy*, 232.
   2. Robert Frost, "The Death of the Hired Man" in *Complete Poems of Robert Frost* (New York: Holt, Rinehart, & Winston, 1964), 53.
   3. *The Word for Us*, trans. Joann Haugerud (Seattle: Coalition on Women and Religion, 1977), Jn. 14:23.
   4. Gerhard Frost, *Homing in the Presence* (Minneapolis: Augsburg, 1978).
   5. G. K. Chesterton, "The House of Christmas" in *Modern Religious Poems*, ed. Jacob Trapp (New York: Harper & Row, 1964), 110.
8. Here Is Faith
   1. Kathryn Ann Lindskoog, *C. S. Lewis: Mere Christian* (Glendale, Cal.: Regal, 1973), 214.
   2. C. S. Lewis, *Dawn Treader*, 215.
9. Here Is Truth
   1. C. S. Lewis, *God in the Dock* (Grand Rapids: Eerdmans, 1970), 58.
   2. Gerhard Frost, *Color of the Night: Reflections on the Book of Job* (Minneapolis: Augsburg, 1977), 35.
   3. Gerhard Frost, *Color of the Night*, 107.
10. Here Is Beauty
   1. Gerhard Frost, *Homing in the Presence*, 49.
   2. Alfred, Lord Tennyson, "In Memoriam A. H. H.," no. 48 in *The Norton Anthology*, 2:1146.
   3. William Wordsworth, "The World Is Too Much with Us" in *The Norton Anthology*, 2:224.
   4. Herbert F. Brokering, *Lord, If* (St. Louis: Concordia, 1977).
11. Here Is Freedom
   1. Molly Dee Rundle, "Choosing Life" in *Images: Women in*

Transition, comp. Janice Grana (Nashville: The Upper Room, 1976), 50.

2. Margaret Mead, *And Keep Your Powder Dry* (New York: Morrow, 1965), 78–79.

12. Here Is Servanthood

1. Brother Lawrence, *The Practice of the Presence of God*, trans. John J. Delaney (Garden City, N.Y.: Doubleday, 1977), 36.

2. Mary R. Schramm, *Gifts of Grace* (Minneapolis: Augsburg, 1982), 119.

3. Dag Hammarskjold, *Markings*, xx.

4. Robert Frost, "Two Tramps in Mudtime" in *Selected Poems of Robert Frost* (San Francisco: Holt, Rinehart, & Winston, 1963), 180.

13. Here Is Joy

1. Marianne Moore, "What Are Years?" in *This Is My Best*, ed. Whit Burnett (New York: Dial Press, 1942), 646.

2. Walter Starcke, *This Double Thread* (New York: Harper & Row, 1967), 45.

3. Brother Lawrence, *Practice of the Presence of God*, 51.

4. Robert Frost, "To Earthward" in *Complete Poems of Robert Frost*, 279.

5. Robert Browning, "Fra Lippo Lippi" in *The Norton Anthology*, 2:964.

14. Here Is Grief

1. Jean Fox Holland, *Images*, comp. Janice Grana, 80.

2. Abraham Heschel, *Prophets*, 147.

3. Eugenia Price, *The Wider Place* (Grand Rapids: Zondervan, 1966), 166.

4. Dona Hoffman, *Yes, Lord* (St. Louis: Concordia, 1974), cover page.

5. Robert Raines, *To Kiss the Joy* (Waco: Word, 1973), 117.

15. Here Is Eternity

1. Rick Gore, "The Once and Future Universe," *National Geographic*, June 1983: 734.

2. Kathryn Ann Lindskoog, *C. S. Lewis*, 136.

3. Edna Hong, "Eternity," *Lutheran Standard*, January 1962, cover page.

Acknowledgments

"Seed" from *Listen to the Green* by Luci Shaw is reprinted by permission of Harold Shaw Publishers. Copyright © 1971 by Luci Shaw.

Selected lines from "The Death of the Hired Man" are from THE POETRY OF ROBERT FROST edited by Edward Connery Lathem. Copyright 1930, 1939, © 1969 by Holt, Rinehart and Winston. Copyright © 1958 by Robert Frost. Copyright © 1967 by Lesley Frost Ballantine. Reprinted by permission of Holt, Rinehart and Winston Publishers and Jonathan Cape Ltd.

Selected lines from MARKINGS by Dag Hammarskjold were translated by Leif Sjoberg and W. H. Auden. Copyright © 1964 by Alfred A. Knopf. Reprinted by permission of the publisher.

Excerpts from WHOLLY HOLY by Herb Brokering, The Brokering Press, 11641 Palmer Road, Minneapolis, MN 55437, are used by permission of the author.

Selected lines by Herb Brokering in LORD, IF © 1977 Concordia Publishing House are used by permission of the publisher.

Selected lines from "The House of Christmas" are reprinted by permission of Dodd, Mead & Co., Inc. from *The Collected Poems of G. K. Chesterton* copyright 1932 by Dodd, Mead & Co., Inc. Copyright renewed 1959 by Oliver Chesterton. Also used by permission of Miss D. E. Collins and Methuen & Co., Ltd. (London).

Excerpt from GOD IN THE DOCK copyright © 1970 by C. S. Lewis Pte Ltd., is reproduced by permission of Curtis Brown Ltd. (London) and Collins Publisher.

Selected lines appearing on page 43 are from *God Is a Verb!* by Marilee Zdenek and Marge Champion, p. 73, copyright © 1974; used by permission of Word Books, Publisher, Waco, Texas 76796.

Excerpts from "Journey of the Magi" in COLLECTED POEMS 1909–1962 by T. S. Eliot; copyright 1936 by Harcourt Brace Jovanovich, Inc.; copyright © 1963, 1964 by T. S. Eliot. Reprinted by permission of Harcourt Brace Jovanovich, Inc., and Faber & Faber Ltd.

ACKNOWLEDGMENTS 127

"Eternity" by Edna Hong is used by permission of the author.

Selected lines from "To Earthward" and "Two Tramps in Mud Time" from THE POETRY OF ROBERT FROST edited by Edward Connery Lathem. Copyright 1923, © 1969 by Holt, Rinehart and Winston. Copyright © 1936, 1951 by Robert Frost. Copyright © 1964 by Lesley Frost Ballantine. Reprinted by permission of Holt, Rinehart and Winston, Publishers and Jonathan Cape Ltd.

"The Prayer of the Lark" from PRAYERS FROM THE ARK by Carmen Bernos de Gosztold. English translation by Rumer Godden. English test copyright © 1962 by Rumer Godden. Reprinted by permission of Viking Penguin Inc.

Excerpt from "The Once and Future Universe," *National Geographic*, June 1983, is reprinted by permission of *National Geographic*.

Selected lines from "What Are Years?" are reprinted with permission of Macmillan Publishing Company from COLLECTED POEMS OF Marianne Moore. Copyright 1941, and renewed 1969 by Marianne Moore. Also reprinted by permission of Faber and Faber Ltd. from THE COMPLETE POEMS OF MARIANNE MOORE.

About the Author

Renée Hermanson is a free-lance writer. Born in Sioux Falls, South Dakota, she has traveled widely with her husband, an air force chaplain, and their five sons. San Antonio, Texas, is now their home.

The author has previously published two books, *Who Speaks for God?* and *Raspberry Kingdom.* Formerly a newspaper editor, she has contributed articles to many periodicals, such as *The Lutheran, Faith at Work,* and *Daughters of Sarah.* A local chapter of Sigma Delta Chi, a professional journalism society, granted Mrs. Hermanson a first place award for a feature story she wrote in 1983. She is currently working as a child development curriculum writer.